LAUREN CONRAD
Style

ALSO BY LAUREN CONRAD

L.A. Candy

Sweet Little Lies
AN L.A. CANDY NOVEL

Sugar and Spice
AN L.A. CANDY NOVEL

LAUREN CONRAD
Style

LAUREN CONRAD

WITH ELISE LOEHNEN

HARPER

An Imprint of HarperCollinsPublishers

Lauren Conrad Style

Text copyright © 2010 by Lauren Conrad

Photos copyright © 2010 by Matt Jones, Howard Huang, Kristian Dowling/Getty Images,

Angela Weiss/Getty Images, and Frank Micelotta/Getty Images

Full credit and copyright information for interior photographs appears on page 223.

Makeup chart illustrations copyright © 2010 by Kerrie Hess

www.harperteen.com

Library of Congress Cataloging-in-Publication Data

Conrad, Lauren.

   Lauren Conrad style / by Lauren Conrad with Elise Loehnen.

     p. cm.

   ISBN 978-0-06-198914-8

   1. Girls' clothing. 2. Dress accessories. 3. Beauty, Personal. 4. Fashion—Psychological aspects. I. Loehnen, Elise. II. Title.

TT562.C66 2010   2010003093

646'.34—dc22   CIP

                                                                                                                   AC

Typography by Sasha Illingworth

10 11 12 13 14   SCP   10 9 8 7 6 5 4 3 2 1

❖

First Edition

This book is dedicated to the wonderful team that spends countless hours doing hair, makeup, and styling to put me together. The same team dedicated so much time and hard work to the development of this book. I am so lucky to work with such talented people and this book would not have been possible without them.

CONTENTS

INTRODUCTION ix

FASHION

BEAUTY

LIFESTYLE

CHAPTER ONE
Building Your Wardrobe

*T*here are a lot of opinions about what every girl should have in her wardrobe, and this usually boils down to a handful of basics. But as essential as these items may be, the thing about basics is they don't have to be basic at all. Each one should suit your personal style. Something as straightforward and simple as a blazer can be interpreted a hundred different ways. To me, it's black and tailored. To you, it might be oversized and navy. To someone else, it's shrunken and embellished. Basics—or what I like to call "key pieces"—are the foundation around which you'll build your wardrobe; you should fall in love with them as hard as you might fall for a wear-it-once gown.

Narrowing your focus when shopping for workhorse pieces is kind of like the complicated dance of back-to-school shopping in middle school. My mom used to always try to lead me toward the things I needed (sneakers, a warm jacket, nice jeans), but all I really wanted were platform sandals; midriff-baring, logo-ed tops; and bedazzled bell-bottoms. (Hey, we've all had poor judgment at one time or another.) Somehow, we managed to meet in the middle and find a happy marriage of practical and, to my thirteen-year-old mind, cooler pieces. In those moments that mattered—school dances, picture day, boy-girl birthday parties—what do you think made it out of my closet? I might not remember the names of all my crushes, but I'll never forget my happy-face-emblazoned baby tee, worn with nice jeans, of course.

I'm not dismissing how much you can come to rely on the perfect blazer or cardigan (in fact, I'm going to talk a lot about these sorts of essentials in this book)—I'm just saying that the dress that makes you feel really beautiful every time you put it on deserves a spot in your stable of can't-live-without-it pieces, too.

I think of the core of my wardrobe as the clothes that I always pack when I travel, because they're comfortable, they're flattering, and they're the items that most make me feel like myself when I'm far from home. It's a good test, actually—to go through your wardrobe and pick out your ten favorite, wear-to-death things, whether it's a white T-shirt, an argyle sweater, or a sequined miniskirt. Boiling it down will give you a pretty good picture of what your personal style is.

Now, nobody can assemble a perfect wardrobe in a day, or even a week—it's a process. I'm constantly looking at magazines and movies for inspiration, and my sense of style evolves all the time. There are always going to be mistakes, which are a part of any fashion evolution. And while I tend to play it pretty safe in public these days (I'm terrified of ending up on the Worst Dressed list), I'm test-driving all sorts of things when I know I'll be flying under the radar for a night. For example, I love crimson lips and layered costume jewelry, even if it's just with a T-shirt and jeans. Unfortunately, red lips don't always photograph well on me and a lot of jewels can look a little over the top. So while it's one of my favorite looks, it only gets its day in the sun at the local bar or a friend's dinner party. You, too, should try out an outfit when pressure is low—don't debut a new top that you're not too sure about on a first date. Wear it out with your friends first so that you know you will feel confident rather than insecure and uncomfortable.

And don't beat yourself up if you buy something that never makes it off the hanger—it happens to the best of us. But you can ensure that it doesn't happen too often if you learn what cuts and styles fit your body and your personality. I've filled the following pages with many useful strategies to help you steer clear of pieces that you may really, really want on the spot but will probably never wear. I'm all about buying what you love, but the goal here is to zero in on that foolproof, confidence-boosting wardrobe.

So let's get started.

KEY PIECES

The following items will help you establish your look. They are all versatile and can be used to build your wardrobe.

LITTLE BLACK DRESS: After nearly a century, the little black dress is still one of the greatest fashion innovations ever (thank you, Coco Chanel!). Finding a well-fitting one is essential. And thankfully, this isn't difficult, since every designer seems to offer at least one variation. Whether yours is A-line or strapless, a wrap style or a standard tank, you can wear it with tights, belted, layered with a cardigan or blazer, or just by itself and make your LBD last through the seasons. When I'm completely at a loss for what to wear, this is one of my favorite go-tos, particularly if I need to look extra-polished. Pair it with ankle booties, stilettos, or flats depending on whether you're looking to dress it up or dress it down. (See p. 98 for five ways I accessorize mine, to make it look completely new every time.)

JEANS: Denim is necessary in any wardrobe. And regardless of your body type, with all of the styles out there, you're sure to find a pair that will look great on you—don't give up in the dressing room until you've found the ones! While you aren't about to wear jeans to a black-tie event (or to prom, for that matter), you can wear them almost anywhere else. A dark wash is the most versatile: Blacks and deep blues are super flattering, and they look fancier, too. (For more on jeans, see chapter 2.)

COLLARED BUTTON-DOWN: Some pieces are just classics, still kicking around eras after they originally made a splash. And while they may get an update every now and then, chances are you can wear the same exact item for at least a decade. I think a collared white shirt looks great on everyone. I wear oversized versions over bikinis at the beach or by the pool, and crisp tailored styles paired with indigo jeans and high heels or tucked into A-line skirts.

SKIRT: A great skirt doesn't generally make a lot of people's must-have lists, but I think it's an essential. When you need to look a little bit fancy, a skirt is perfect. Sure, dresses accomplish the same thing (with the added convenience of being an entire outfit in one piece), but skirts are more versatile. You'll get a lot more bang for your buck wearing a skirt with flats and T-shirts for a casual look, or paired with a blouse and heels for an evening out.

BOOTS: Whether they are embellished motorcycle style, flat riding boots, or platformed knee-highs, the perfect pair is based entirely on personal preferences. And boots definitely come in handy, particularly for in-between and colder seasons. But remember, they often face the roughest weather, so don't forget to get your boots treated before taking them for a stroll.

WHITE AND BLACK TOPS: Many outfits I wear include some version of a black or white shirt. Whether it's cotton, jersey, silk, or chiffon, it's the perfect example of what a key piece represents: It's not necessarily the stand-out item in the outfit, but it's the glue holding the entire look together without detracting from whatever the actual centerpiece may be. I've worn white or black tops tucked into pencil skirts, draped over cutoffs, bloused over a full, printed skirt, or with simple jeans. They never fail me.

BLACK HEELS: I own a pair of sky-high black heels that look fabulous but by the end of the night I'm walking like I have a broken toe or really need to pee. So I bought a pair with a more sensible heel height. They're not spectacular—but they're comfortable and therefore practical. Eventually, I managed to find something in between—from that mystical land of comfortable and stunning footwear. They have a five-inch heel but come complete with a hidden platform, so they feel less intense. I love them so much I've had them resoled twice.

BLAZER: A well-cut jacket is a great layering piece, plus it can pull any outfit together and make it look more polished. I love a shrunken blazer with a white tee and skinny jeans for daytime, and an oversized boyfriend blazer paired with a feminine-looking minidress at night. When you're shopping for your blazer, you can select a simple one in a classic cut or one that's got a little something special, whether it's embellishment, fun stitching, or an interesting lining.

COAT: One downside of living in sunny California is that I don't often get to reach for a winter coat, even though they're one of my favorite things to shop for. Everyone looks great in a coat. You can throw one on and walk down the street looking stylish (you could have your ducky pajamas on underneath and nobody would know). And while a coat's main purpose is to keep you warm, you can score one that's fashionable *and* functional. Go for a bold color or one with embellishments (half of mine sport at least one bow somewhere).

For my last birthday, I headed to Vegas with ten of my closest friends. I was ready for an unforgettable evening, except for one thing: I didn't have anything to wear! (I promise.) While everyone else was getting excited for our weekend of fun, I couldn't even begin to think about enjoying it until I had the perfect dress. My friends thought I was being silly. My boyfriend couldn't wrap his head around my dilemma. (I had to draw a surfing analogy for him, which is the best way to make him relate to any fashion crisis.) So two hours before I had to leave for the airport, I made a frantic trip through Saks. And then I saw it. It was beautiful. I wasn't even bothered by the fact that it weighed 4.5 pounds. (Seriously, I weighed it on my scale.) And then I looked at the price. Gasp! Out of sheer embarrassment, I won't reveal what I spent that day, but I went to Vegas and had a fabulous birthday in a fabulous dress—that I never wore again. Was it a smart purchase? Not so much. But sometimes it's okay to spend a little more than you planned if it makes you feel special.

WHERE TO SPLURGE, AND WHERE TO SAVE

Creating versatile garments that don't cost a lot of money was really important when I designed my Kohl's line. You don't always have to splurge to look good. The trick to building your wardrobe is knowing *what* to splurge on. Should you spend $500 on a trendy fringed dress that you hope to have an excuse to wear . . . someday? No! But going a little crazy on a pair of black platform sandals that you'll get a lot of use out of over time is understandable. It really comes down to a cost-per-wear situation—a $300 dress that you can wear to ten parties becomes much more affordable than a $60 dress you'll wear once and toss.

You don't need to spend a fortune on layering tops (drapey tops cut from rayon work really well—and look expensive, too) or T-shirts and jeans. There are some pieces—a hand-tailored jacket, a perfectly draped dress, a cashmere sweater, or a silk blouse—where you can see the price that you paid in the quality of the fabric and the handiwork, but if something inexpensive looks good to you, it probably looks good to everyone else.

LAUREN'S GO-TO PIECES

Key pieces look different in every girl's closet, so here's a glance at mine.

T-SHIRTS: Enough said, right? I like mine a touch slouchy and lightweight. I also like sneaking a T-shirt into a nicer outfit, like with a statement miniskirt, because it pulls the look together without stealing any of the spotlight. (For help with finding the perfect tee, see p. 33).

BLACK MINIDRESS: My black, tiered Stella McCartney dress wasn't as short on the rack; I had my tailor transform it into a mini (more on that on p. 104). I've worn it with a strand of classic pearls, paired with tights and a blazer, and under a shrunken leather jacket with gladiator heels. One dress, so many looks.

SKINNY JEANS: Black, indigo, light-washed, distressed . . . I own every variation of skinny jeans (or, as I call them, skinnies). They may not be the jean for everyone, but they're definitely my go-to cut. I wear them with a tank top and sandals, or tucked into boots with loads of layers. They are the most versatile item in my closet. My favorite pairs are from J. Brand, Urban Outfitters, and Levi's.

MAXI DRESSES: Maybe it's the Southern Californian in me, but come summer, I can often be found in a maxi dress. They're super casual but also dramatic, and if the waist hits just right (empire is the best for me), then I think they're exceptionally flattering, too.

OVERSIZED SWEATERS: Whether they're worn to the airport with leggings or layered over a sundress, I love sweaters. Because I live in California, mine are usually lightweight. I spend so many nights in strapless dresses that are so tight they literally take my breath away, all I want to do in my off-moments is slip into something comfortable. And to my mind, a beautiful sweater is equal parts glamorous and pajama-like. Scoop-neck, V-neck, or cardigan, they all play leading roles in my closet.

BLACK HEELS: If my devotion to black platform heels isn't already clear, let me confirm it here: I own countless pairs of shoes, many of them colorful and many of them embellished, but I come back to my favorite black platform heels at least once a week. I wear them to dress up jeans or to look good (and tall) on the red carpet. Regardless of the occasion, they totally lengthen out my legs and have never let me down. (These are the ones I've had resoled twice; I intend to keep them alive as long as possible.)

CHAPTER TWO

The All-American Uniform: Jeans and T-shirts

*I*f you can track down the perfect pair of jeans for your figure and a handful of T-shirts that fit you well, you'll have made a serious dent in building your ideal wardrobe. There's really nothing that will serve as a better foundation for putting together great outfits.

How, you may ask, do I state this with such authority? Besides the fact that I live it almost every day, the history of this all-American uniform is almost as old as America itself. (As a concept, it dates back to late-eighteenth-century France where they made a fabric called "serge" . . . in the town of Nîmes. Serge de Nîmes. Get it? Denim . . .) It's evolved considerably over the years: At first, denim made for some pretty intense workwear (dungarees!); then in the '50s it became edgy and cool (think of James Dean's swoony outfit of choice in *Rebel Without a Cause* or, sigh, the wardrobe in *Grease*); and then ultimately, it went mainstream. Until about 1990 or so, when it reached a whole new level: Designers finally decided to give it their full attention and created a gigantic market. Denim for everybody!!! There are hundreds of brands out there now, where once there were only a few popular ones (Levi's, Wrangler, and the Gap).

The upside: a wealth of great options. The downside: It can be difficult to parse through all those brands and styles to find your perfect fit. But it's out there! And it is imperative that you find it. A great pair of jeans can do more for your butt and legs than any contouring bodywear—and jeans are so supremely effortless, versatile, and easy to style, that they can singularly make getting dressed a breeze.

Another timeless item, of course, is the T-shirt. As with denim, the T-shirt had a humble beginning, only to evolve into a fashionable staple (with its own iconic movie moments—picture James Dean again). What began as an undergarment—white cotton and crewneck—is now available in any imaginable color, cut, or style. There are enough options to induce a panic attack, but through trial and error you're sure to zero in on the cut that works best for you. I like mine thin (but not transparent), loose, and long enough to hit at the very top of my thigh.

JEANS

FINDING THE RIGHT PAIR

Unless you're at a store that provides the benefit of a three-way mirror, it's crucial to bring a trusted friend with you when shopping for jeans. Finding the perfect pair is a bit like running a marathon—you'll be disappointed if you give in before you reach the end, which in this case means having the best pair in hand. This involves trying on a ton. That flattering fit is so elusive, in fact, that I buy multiples when I finally find it. Jean companies tinker with cut, fabric, and shape from season to season, so even if the style name remains the same, they likely won't be an exact match. And if you wear denim as much as I do, you know the heartbreaking tragedy of wearing out your favorite pair. So don't risk the disappointment of not being able to replace them by stocking up while you can!

Almost all denim these days has a bit of stretch built in, which is key for creating a nice line for your legs. Plus, denim with stretch is way more comfortable than old-fashioned, super-thick denim. But keep this in mind when you're trying on jeans: Especially if they have 2 percent or more of stretch (check the tag inside), they should be as tight as humanly possible because the fabric will ultimately "give" a lot. As long as they look good and you can zip and button them—and breathe!—they're not too tight. While you're in the dressing room, do some lunges and squats to stretch them out a tiny bit. If you buy them too loose, you'll have to wash them between every wear, which gets frustrating and can cause premature fading. I like to wear jeans for long periods of time between washes because I think it breaks them in a lot faster.

My legs aren't particularly long, so all jeans drag on the floor when I'm in the dressing room. Fold them under until they're the proper length (this means you need to decide whether you'll be wearing them with heels or flats) so you can get a sense of what they'll look like hemmed.

Before I drop off my jeans at the tailor for hemming (see p. 25 if you want to attempt this yourself), I turn them inside out (to protect the color) and wash them first so that any shrinkage is accounted for. It may seem obvious, but make sure you bring the shoes you'll want to wear with your jeans to the tailor—this is a much better maneuver than standing on your tippy toes trying to approximate where the hem should hit. And if you don't know which shoes to pair with your jeans, turn to p. 27.

THE KEY TO POCKET PLACEMENT

The position and size of the back pockets can dramatically affect what your butt looks like in jeans—smaller pockets will make it look bigger, ones that are too close together will make it look wider. In general, choose pockets that are standard in size, which angle in slightly—they're the most flattering.

DENIM DISTRESSING

I'm generally a fan of jeans with a cleaner wash—I like pristine blues and blacks, without any machine-made whiskering or intentional, fake-looking aging. But as I wear my jeans in, I take no issue with marks

A Note About Rises . . .

Do you remember the time when jeans were cut with ridiculously low rises, revealing every girl in the land's underwear preference? Those days were kind of the worst. Besides requiring me to make a constant lower-back check to ensure I wasn't flashing the general public, I lived in constant fear of literally falling out of my pants.

Because that actually happened to me.

At a school assembly.

I was wearing three-inch-rise jeans from Gap that had absolutely no stretch when I was selected during a pep rally to play a game of Extreme Twister in front of the whole school. I was already in a difficult position when . . . I attempted "left foot yellow" and my entire butt popped out of my pants. (Note to self: Don't make enemies on the yearbook staff. . . . They have the power to include these moments in the end-of-year video. You know who you are!)

from legitimate wear and tear. They can add tons of character. And, in fact, I have a few secrets for speeding the process along.

GENTLE ABRASIONS: Costume designers have a couple methods for making clothing look old. The first is trisodium phosphate, or TSP, a powerful chemical agent that breaks down the fiber in clothing (you add it to the washing machine), but you should probably be a professional to use it (or at least practice on things that you don't care about!). If you want the effect to be subtle and strategically placed, go with the second method: Use a small piece of sandpaper or a cheese grater to distress the fabric. Just make sure to concentrate on areas that make sense, wear-wise.

BLEACH: Unless you want an acid-washed pair, go gentle with bleach—you can always add more. I only use this approach on lighter-wash jeans, so the effect is a bit more understated. Dilute a tiny bit of bleach in a lot of water and dip a toothbrush (not one you intend to use in your mouth!) in the solution—then brush your thumb against the bristles, flicking the liquid onto the fabric. Once you're satisfied, wash immediately; otherwise, the bleach will continue to slowly eat away at the fabric.

MAINTAINING THE WASH OF YOUR JEANS

The downside of really richly hued jeans (i.e., pitch black or deep blue) is that the designers likely had to over-dye them to reach the shade. And while this is a great look for your legs (the darker they are, the more likely the pants are to flatter), it can be devastating for white couches, suede bags, and T-shirts. Be careful that the dye doesn't transfer onto something you love! (I once ruined a nude-colored Chanel bag the second time I wore it, by way of dark denim.)

TROUSER-STYLE JEANS: This is another popular work option because they tend to be slightly higher in the rise and have a proper pants-style closure (i.e., a tab rather than just a button). I like tucking an oxford into these and layering a thin cardigan over. I try to avoid anything too high in the waist—wear them if you're inclined, but I have yet to see a girl I think they truly flatter.

SHOE CHOICES: Because the pant leg will cover the shoe, you can go for a wide range of options (including heels that are a little beaten up). If you want to wear your jeans with sneakers (like a Jack Purcell Converse or a Ked), this is a good pant to choose since the material will conceal them. Plus, the dressed-up nature of the jeans counters the casualness of the shoe.

BOOT-CUT JEANS: These were pretty revolutionary when they hit the scene because they're flattering on almost any body shape. This is primarily because the slight flare at the bottom balances out any curviness in the hips. Make sure that they're the perfect length, though. If there's a puddle of material on the floor, they have the opposite-of-flattering effect and will just make you look big.

SHOE CHOICES: So named because of their versatility with boots, these are good with any sort of heel, booted or otherwise. Definitely skip anything that needs to go *over* the pant leg, though, since your calf area will be swimming in material.

BOYFRIEND JEANS: The super-baggy jean is one of those trends that reemerges every few years—and for good reason. They're unbelievably comfortable and can also be quite flattering, so long as you balance out the proportion. I know they're essentially the sweats of the denim world, but you have to pair them with a fitted or tailored top so that you don't look sloppy.

SHOE CHOICES: I normally wear a thin sandal or simple ballet flat with this style. Because this cut is super casual and baggy, you might need a heel to make it a bit fancier—plus, the extra height will help you pull off all that fabric.

'70S-INSPIRED FLARE JEANS: The key to this particular trend is to make sure that you leave them super long and find the shoes to match. Normally I like to leave about an inch between jeans and the ground. As a general rule, these should literally skim the earth. This is a great choice if your legs are on the shorter side, since all that fabric will create the illusion of longer legs.

SHOE CHOICES: Anything with a really, really high heel, from a platform to an ankle bootie. I love the idea of an earthy, woven wedge.

T-SHIRTS

HOW SHEER IS TOO SHEER?

T-shirts are so simple in concept, but they can be a total disaster in execution. I love that designers are paying so much attention to them: There are now hundreds of options, many of which feature loads of innovations fabric-wise, but all of this choice can make it a bit more difficult to whittle the field down. And just as denim makers took the "low-rise" craze a little too far a few years ago, T-shirt manufacturers have gone a little crazy in their quest for the perfect paper-thin material.

Many of the T-shirts out there these days are just too sheer to flatter. A quick field-test while shopping for T-shirts is to stretch the fabric over your hand—if your palm is visible underneath, then all those parts you might want to conceal on your stomach or sides will be visible, too. Granted, this doesn't mean that you need the super-thick versions of yesteryear, but the T-shirt should have some opacity, and maybe a tiny bit of structure. You want it to glide over your curves, not cling. When you find the perfect T-shirt—soft, long, slouchy, concealing—buy multiples!

FLATTERING SLEEVE LENGTHS

It's funny how dramatically sleeve length can affect the look of a T-shirt. (If you don't believe me, roll your shirtsleeves while looking in a mirror.) You want the sleeve to hit at either a thin point of your arm or at a point where your muscle has peaked and is starting to dwindle. If the sleeve stops at a point on your arm where the muscle is extending out, it will make it look much bigger than it actually is.

HOW TO LAYER T-SHIRTS

If you accidently bought some aforementioned overly sheer tees, hold on to them for layering purposes. I love a sheer T-shirt under a strapless dress (it makes them totally appropriate for day). You could also wear one under a second, equally sheer shirt. The bottom layer should be slightly longer than the top layer.

HOW TO KEEP WHITES WHITE

There's some sort of chemical reaction between sweat, deodorant, and cotton that creates those unsightly yellow stains. You can attack the problem with a few different approaches (but skip the bleach since it doesn't help at all here). One trick is to soak the stained area in hydrogen peroxide (you can dilute it in water), another is to pop an aspirin or two into the washing machine (wait until it's full of water), or you could soak the offending T-shirt in a solution of vinegar and water (1 tablespoon of vinegar to 1 cup of water).

CHAPTER THREE
The Hunt: How to Shop

*L*ike you would on any day spent in the wilderness, you should have a good plan when preparing to shop. It's important to know not only what you are hunting but the best places to look—and the proper attire and appropriate ammunition are key, too. Whether you're narrowing in on the coolest crocodile clutch or a killer pair of Gucci heels, a lack of planning might just leave you empty-handed or worse, totally dissatisfied. So lace up your boots, polish your credit cards, and get ready for the hunt.

Make it easier on yourself by wearing comfortable shoes—a good day of shopping involves a lot of legwork. If the weather is nice, wear a skirt or dress. (Taking jeans on and off is tiring . . . and don't get me started on tights!) I usually add a tank top layer into the mix, too, because even though boutiques hate it, if there's a line for the dressing room, you can just slip blouses and sweaters on in the middle of the store.

I prefer to shop alone so that my decision-making process doesn't get muddled by someone else's personal style. For example, my best friend and I have very different taste. Whenever we shop together we toss a lot of loving barbs, like "Yeah, that's cute . . . if you want to look like a circus runaway." In the past, I've let myself be influenced by other people's opinions, but these days, I really don't want to be talked out of buying something I love just because it's not to someone else's taste. That said, the right set of trusted eyes can be handy. A good shopping partner should be honest but kind—with a working knowledge of your closet. That is, someone who can steer you away from those items you already have a ton of, whether it is jeans or turquoise party tops. And someone who can clue you in to the fact that something isn't flattering without destroying your self-esteem.

It's key to figure out how much you're willing to spend before you set foot in any stores. This budget should define what you think the demands of your shopping list require (shopping for basic tees would mean a smaller budget, a new winter coat would mean a bigger one), and the outer limit of what you can afford. If you tend to get carried away with credit cards, bring cash instead. It's much harder to hand over $20 bills than it is to keep swiping plastic. And it will make you think very carefully before you commit to any purchases, which is good news for your wallet *and* your closet. (You don't want to overload your wardrobe with impulse buys that make it difficult to see the pieces you actually wear all the time.)

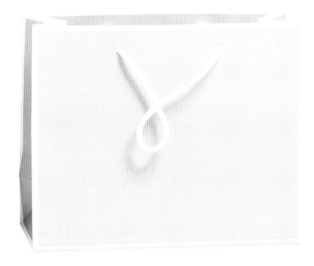

TACKLING DEPARTMENT STORES
AND MASS CHAINS

As a wise woman once said, always do a quick lap before committing to a location. (Yes, I just quoted Cher from *Clueless*.) She was talking about a party, but I think this also applies to a large department store. I usually cruise around the main floor before circling back and grabbing the pieces that caught my eye the first time around. You should go with your immediate instinct, because if an item jumps out at you from the racks, it will also jump out at you in your own closet. If you shop as often as I do (Hey now! I have to keep up on trends for a variety of projects—it's rough, but someone's got to do it . . .), quick, instinctual shopping is a good way to stop yourself from buying too much. When I'm on the prowl for understated basics, I take the time to flip through the racks. This is particularly important if said key piece is black or navy—it can be really hard to see the detailing within a mass of other similarly hued pieces.

Skipping Regret

Although the dreaded "why did I buy that?" experience is all too common, at one point or another we all experience the "why *didn't* I buy it?" blues, too. That dress that fit perfectly but was slightly too expensive. The shoes that you thought were too trendy, only to be trolling eBay looking for them two seasons later since you can't get them out of your mind. I've come up with a system to minimize these regrets: Most stores don't have a problem holding items for a few hours, so when I find myself doing the "do I really need this?" dance, I simply put the garment on hold for the day and continue shopping. If I still want it a few hours later, I swing by and pick it up. If I've forgotten about it or feel even a tiny bit of relief at the money saved, then I don't bother.

DRESSING ROOM STRATEGY

I don't know if it's the stale, over-circulated air back there, but dressing rooms tend to be soul crushing and energy draining. (Small space + scary lighting = my version of a tiny hell.) So enter prepared! Bring multiple sizes so you don't have to head out for more, and try things on in the appropriate order (don't leave yourself topless, for example) if you're planning to leave the fitting room for an impromptu fashion show for your friends.

If you tend to lose steam halfway through the trying-on process, tackle the most intensive pieces first (dresses, jeans) and save the easy-peasy ones for last (cardigans, blazers, coats). Also, prioritize your favorites: If you find something on the racks you sort of like but aren't sure about, bring it with you. If you can't muster the energy to try it on after you've worked your way through everything else, you'll have answered the question of whether you need it after all.

It's important to sit down in any pants/jeans/skirts/dresses you're trying on because you'll want to know if they're comfortable if you need to sit for an extended period, and if pants ride too low in the back or skirts and dresses rise too high. It's also a good idea to leave the dressing room area to both get an idea of how a garment moves on you and see it from another perspective or in different lighting: Unless I have a friend with me, I always make sure to check myself out in front of at least two mirrors (some are likely skinny, others won't be so generous). There's nothing worse than getting home and trying on a purchase, only to find out that you were conned into thinking it was flattering!

AVOIDING IMPULSE PURCHASES AT HUGE, WALLET-FRIENDLY STORES

The one thing I strongly believe should not cost a fortune are layering tops, so I can often be found in that section of H&M or Forever 21, stocking up on tanks and shirts made from synthetic fabrics like rayon or modal. They tend to be really swingy, and the fact that they don't cling is super flattering. If you're buying key pieces like that, forge ahead, regret-free.

Sometimes, though, a little restraint would've helped me out. I'm sure I'm not alone here, but I've wandered into a big chain store—whether it's American Apparel, H&M, or Topshop—only to wander out hundreds of dollars poorer. I'm still not sure exactly how it happens. One minute I'm admiring a pretty $20 top and the next thing I know I'm standing at the cash register with a pile of clothing two feet tall. Now, mathematics wasn't my strongest subject (please hold the obvious joke here), but the logic seems rather elementary. Lots of small numbers equal a big number, and yet I'm always standing at the register scratching my head . . . $300?!?! And while I've found some great things in these accidental sprees that I've worn to death, I've also managed to fill my closet with many "did-I-really-need-this?" items. I don't usually make these irrational choices when the clothes are more expensive—only when they are so affordable that there's seemingly no choice to be made. Danger! Don't buy something just because the price is right.

TREND TESTING

Before you commit to a scary or expensive trend, you can test-drive it with a budget-friendly option. For example, before splashing out for a leather bomber jacket, try a faux leather version that costs $70 first. If you decide you love it, chances are the real deal that's going to last for years and years is a sound investment.

REAL   DEAL

CHAPTER FOUR
Mastering Your Closet

PEEP-TOE: These are sexy because they're subtly revealing. Look for them in a pretty, feminine color, like a soft gray or mauve.

EMBELLISHED: Think of this pair as the perfect counterpoint to a simple black dress, so consider jewels or sequins, or a fun, bright color.

GLADIATOR: These are a fun option because they're a tougher version of a sandal. But be sure to pay close attention when you try them on because they can be uncomfortable around your ankles.

BOOTS: Whether you prefer heeled or flat, pick a classic, straightforward boot, something you love now but could also see yourself loving two years from now. A good pair of boots can be costly, so just be sure to spend wisely.

DOUBLE THE LIFE
OF YOUR SHOES

I know it's totally heartbreaking, but if you buy a pair of shoes that you'd like to keep for a long time, you absolutely have to take them to a cobbler first. (Okay, admission: I can't help myself and usually wear them once before doing this.) Spend the extra $20 or so to have a rubber sole added—they'll last twice as long.

TROUBLESOME ANKLES

Having shorter legs means that any sort of shoe that cuts me off at the ankle is tough. (Jealous, right?) This includes everything from ankle booties to gladiator sandals to T-strap heels. If it's approaching the problematic area, the trick is to find something that dips slightly in front, whether by design or because it's a little loose and drapey. Definitely avoid a strap or swath of leather that creates a straight line, which will completely cut you off. If I fall in love with a pair that doesn't do my legs any favors, I purchase the shoes in black and wear them with black tights to create a longer line.

Tricks of the Trade: What Your Cobbler Can Do for You

It can be a difficult process, but shop around for a great cobbler. (Ask your favorite department store or shoe boutique who they use in the area.) I can't tell you how many times I've been told that something can't be fixed (a snapped heel, for example), only to find a pro who makes the injured shoe look brand-new. Besides basic repairs like retapping heels or adding rubber soles, a good cobbler should be able to stretch too-tight-in-the-calf boots or add special insoles to make a pair that's too big fit. (There are drugstore solutions for this, too, though they don't work quite as well.) I've also had my shoe guy re-dye ballet flats that have seen better days into a slate gray or black. This is particularly key if you have a pet who has fine taste in shoes: My dog Chloe loves to chew off heels, and I've been lucky enough to find a cobbler who can bring them back to life.

BAGS

There are the bags we love, and the bags we actually use—and then there are those that can be both. Keep in mind that purses are dreamed up by artists, not architects, which means that style *always* trumps function in the design process. While you want a tote that's beautiful, it should be practical, too. If you stick to a fairly conservative dress code, a richly hued bag is a great way to make your outfit a little more exciting.

SHOPPING FOR BAGS 101

First things first, assess how much the bag weighs when empty. If you're anything like me, you schlep around significantly more than a day's essentials, which can get heavy! So make sure that you're starting with a piece of leather that doesn't already weigh five pounds. And beware of lots of extraneous hardware—I love the look, too, but it can make a straightforward purse totally unmanageable. (Making your boyfriend carry it for you is not a good solution!) While still at the store, take out all the paper stuffing, and put the contents of your own bag in there. Does it all fit? Does the bag hang well?

While you're at it, make sure you're considering all those minor—but important—details of your life. Do you need to carry a computer? (Pick something with sturdy handles.) Do you walk a lot? (A cross-body satchel is a good solution for hauling a lot of weight over a long period of time, plus it allows you to keep your hands free.) Do you leave pens uncapped? (Go for something black or navy, which will conceal stains.)

TRICKY MATERIALS— HANDLING SUEDE AND PATENT LEATHER

Suede is always a super-soft choice, but one of its downsides is that it can pick up color transfers from almost anything (beware of those over-dyed jeans, for example). It can also get a little nubby when it wears out. You can fix this by brushing over the affected area with a nail file. Patent leather tends to be pretty sturdy, though it can pick up stains—easy to remove via a cotton swab doused in nail polish remover.

A BAG FOR EVERY OCCASION

Bags come in different shapes and sizes. You should own an everyday bag that works with your lifestyle, but you can't wear your everyday bag *every* day, so it's good to have options for when a bag swap is required.

EVERYDAY BAG: Choose one that's comfortable to carry, fits all your things, *and* looks stylish.

CLUTCH: For nights when I want to travel light, I love a clutch. It's small, classic, and feminine. It's generally worn with something special so I opt for one in a neutral color— that way it doesn't steal the spotlight.

EVENING: I'm always careful not to go too tiny when it comes to an evening bag: I will never be that girl who can survive for a night with a credit card, ID, and a handful of twenties. It has to be large enough to contain all my essentials, plus lip gloss, a camera, and my phone.

OVERSIZED CLUTCH: Previously relegated to evening hours only, an oversized clutch is one of my main daytime go-tos: Its smaller size requires an edit, which means I'm not hauling around lots of unnecessary things . . . like five magazines.

LARGE: A large bag should be spacious enough to contain everything you need during the day without the threat of stretching out the leather or snapping the strap.

TRAVEL: The best travel bags can accommodate a change of clothes, a good book, and a computer—not too precious but chic enough to work as a day bag once I arrive at my destination.

JEWELRY

With enough willpower, you could compile a pretty comprehensive clothing and accessory wardrobe in a short amount of time. But that's not always the case when it comes to jewelry. It's nice when shoes and clothes have sentimental value (you know, the dress you wore on an amazing first date or the "lucky" shoes you're convinced landed you your first job), but most just don't. With the jewelry that you wear every day, though—which admittedly has absolutely no utilitarian function—there's probably some underlying story that makes it special.

I have a huge cache of costume jewelry that I dip into all the time, but for the most part, it's not the stuff I wear on a daily basis. Those slots are reserved for the pieces that matter, which are best accumulated over time. Jewelry is different for everyone, so some people treasure their big diamond studs, simple silver bangle, or delicate gold chain strung with charms that took years to collect. I'm always reaching for a familiar ring or necklace when I'm nervous or far from home. It might sound cheesy, but it's nice to have tokens nearby from people you care about. Of course, you can't always count on all your jewelry to be gifts; sometimes you want to buy a little something for yourself—and that's nice, too.

LAYERING JEWELRY 101

When it comes to jewelry, my first instinct is the more the merrier. That said, if I'm making a big statement around my neck, I'll downplay my earrings—or wear no earrings at all. There's something about an oversized earring/necklace combo that seems dated—plus, they tend to compete. In the same vein, if I've added an armful of bracelets, I skip rings on that hand. Really, it depends if you are wearing a statement piece or if you want a little bit of everything. If your necklace, bangles, and rings are a little more dainty and don't fight with one another then don't be afraid to put everything on together.

EARRINGS

Of all types of jewelry, these are the most important things to try on before you buy. A pair that looks delicate on a friend might completely dominate your face, depending on the shape and size of your head. I suggest investing in one small everyday pair of earrings, whether they are little diamond studs or small gold hoops, and a handful of larger pieces for special occasions.

NECKLACES

Layering necklaces shouldn't be a complex undertaking. It should really just be a happy jumble around your neck. Granted, if you get more than four necklaces going, they'll probably get tangled. You can avoid this by layering necklaces that are of different lengths, from super long, almost navel-grazing chains to something that hits right at the clavicle. I keep some spare chains around at the three main lengths—12", 14", and 18"—so that if I need to swap out some pendants, I can.

BRACELETS

This is a great opportunity to mix more precious and delicate pieces with tougher, bolder pieces. A few simple gold bangles, some chains, and even a friendship bracelet all look great together. I love layering an eclectic mix of jewels on my arm.

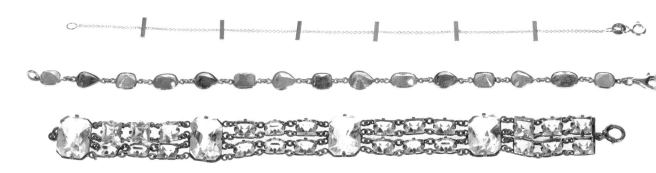

FAKE IT UNTIL YOU MAKE IT: CHEAP JEWELRY

When it comes to fun, on-trend jewelry, you don't have to spend a fortune: Forever 21, Alltherageonline.com, and your local jewelry wholesale district are all great resources. (Despite the implications of the latter, they normally all sell to the public.)

And when it comes to full-on diamonds, you don't need gigantic, bling-y studs, either. There are tons of great alternatives. Don't get fixated on karat count and instead go for a piece of jewelry that feels like you.

DIAMOND CHIPS: A lot of jewelers use flat, diamond chips to create the same effect—for a fraction of the price.

PASTE: Readily available on eBay and in antique stores and flea markets, paste jewelry began to crop up in the 1800s. It's leaded glass, backed on foil, and painted to look like the real thing. You can find extremely intricate and gorgeous pieces, which still cost almost nothing compared to the real thing.

CUBIC ZIRCONIA: If you want some straightforward studs, CZ is a good alternative. Don't go crazy on the size—the more moderate they are, the more realistic they'll appear. (These are nice if you're constantly losing an earring like me.)

Keeping Jewelry Organized

There have been some sad times in my life when my necklaces have become so tangled that I haven't worn them in months—it can take hours to separate a pile! Fortunately, I've stumbled upon a few fail-safe ways for keeping them organized. (And see p. 184 for tips on traveling tangle-free.)

JEWELRY TREE: You can find these at stores like Pottery Barn and Urban Outfitters. Essentially, they're designed to look like an Eiffel Tower or spindly tree or some other structure that has lots of little arms. Give each necklace its own branch or prong, just to ensure that they don't mingle.

PINS: Go to the craft store and pick up some long pushpins with pearlized ends and stick them into the wall. (This doesn't have to be perfect.) They're strong enough to hold up delicate chains, and they create a really pretty pattern on the wall.

BEDPOSTS: Use your jewelry as a display—I drape necklaces over doorknobs and bedposts in my bedroom.

GLOVES

I think a lot of us associate little ladylike leather driving gloves with our grandmothers, but this so shouldn't be the case! I love a brightly colored pair with a black, brown, or white jacket. If you're walking around on a chilly day, nobody gets to see the outfit under your coat, so this is your best way to show off your sense of style (and keep your fingers nice and toasty).

SCARVES

There's been a gigantic scarf resurgence in the last few years—and for good reason. They're one of the easiest ways to add a dose of color, texture, and pattern to an outfit—like a statement necklace but comfortable and warm! One of the best things about them is that they don't cost a fortune, unless you're springing for a fancy silk version or oversized cashmere wrap. I tend to stockpile the long, thin ones since they're the easiest to wear. Reserve louder prints for simpler outfits, whereas neutral-hued options work with almost anything.

ALTERNATE USES FOR SILK SCARVES

It can get frustrating to keep a silk scarf around your neck (it's slippery!), so I like to fold mine into a thin strip and tie it onto the handles of a neutral bag. It's an elegant way to add a touch of color and pattern. You can do a knot, or a bow—don't be too precious about it!

Sometimes I use one as a hair accessory. Choose a relatively narrow scarf for this (if there's too much material it gets a little bulky): Fold it until it's about three inches wide, and then place it in your hair as you would a headband. Tie it underneath your hair, and voilà! A chic spin on the bandanna!

THE UNEXPECTED ACCESSORY: NAIL POLISH!

I know it seems like it shouldn't quite qualify (it is a beauty product, after all), but I think of nail polish as an outfit finisher. When I'm wearing clothing that's neutral and understated, I often opt for something a little out there on my nails, whether it's a near-black red, metallic purple, or even a neon pink. It's a great way to play with color without committing in a bigger way, and it's a fun way to test-drive a trend (yes, there are even trends when it comes to nail polish) without feeling like you're wearing it all over your body. It's easy to take off, it flatters every skin tone, and it's cheap! What could be better?

CHAPTER SIX

Getting Dressed: The Fun Part

*W*hen you're on a reality TV show "playing" yourself, it's important to figure out what your personal style is—and quickly. It's even more important to figure out what's flattering! As I mentioned earlier, there was nobody to help me. During my five years on TV, I never used a stylist for filming: It was entirely my responsibility to make sure that I didn't repeat an outfit. That doesn't mean I never wore the same thing twice, though. My favorite skinny jeans, high-waisted skirts, and loose white tees made countless appearances—I just had to make them look completely new. For this, I developed a few useful tricks.

The first was to look for ideas everywhere—editorial spreads, street-style blogs, the girls brunching alongside me on Saturday mornings—and to take quick notes or tear out pages of looks from magazines that I wanted to try at home. It's a good strategy for finding inspiration, and for stealing ingenious styling tricks (like pinning a handful of vintage badges to an otherwise straightforward blazer or putting together a completely monochromatic outfit). Plus, gathering a ton of different images will help you get a good sense of what it is that you like. (You might find that every single thing you respond to visually is preppy, or Victorian, or some combination of the two.)

The second trick was to grab a fashionable friend and a digital camera and start styling and snapping. When you're feeling inspired, you'd be amazed at how many different looks you can wring out of just a handful of pieces over the course of an afternoon. (If you're stumped, read on—I've done a lot of the legwork for you in the following pages.) If you figure out fifteen outfits, you have fifteen remedies for those days when you feel like you have nothing to wear (and they happen . . . way too often!). Now, if I were a different person and much, *much* more organized, I would have created a continuity binder, which is what costume designers and wardrobe assistants rely on when they're shooting a movie. (Scenes are never shot in order and they need to keep close track of when an actress wears each outfit so the various scenes slot together seamlessly.) Oh, how I wish I had documented what I wore on *The Hills*—it would have been the best reference guide to my closet, ever. But that said, it doesn't have to be complicated: Perfect an outfit, take a picture or jot down some notes, and you're good to go!

And finally, I learned to stop thinking about a garment on the rack as an almost sacred, untouchable thing. Sure, some things are just right the way they were made. But that's the rare exception. For the most part, everything needs a tiny bit of customization, whether it's as simple as rolling the sleeves on a shirt, or as extreme as cutting a vintage dress in two and just wearing the skirt. Point is, getting dressed shouldn't be about perfection; it should be liberating and fun, in the same way that digging into your dress-up trunk when you were a little girl was the best way to spend an afternoon. To be honest, I still have a dress-up trunk, and not only for Halloween. I'm always adding a silk scarf here or a vintage hairpin there. I've collected costume jewelry for years and have more than I can wear (see p. 81 for more on this).

So, if you have a big event—an interview, a party, a first date—don't wait to figure out your outfit until the last minute. This just leads to panic attacks. Start thinking about it days in advance so you can luxuriate in the process—getting dressed is really the best part!

FOOLPROOF OUTFITS

Here's a handy cheat sheet to some of my go-to Date and Weekend looks. (For work and school outfits, see chapter 9, and for party suggestions see chapter 11.)

DATE NIGHT

First dates are one of the most fun—and most stressful—occasions to dress for: What you choose to wear says a lot about you, so it's important to figure out exactly what message you want to send.

A lot of people say that you should look good while simultaneously looking like you didn't try. I'm all for low-key elegance, but I think that making a visible effort is the right move. When you think about it, isn't it sort of rude not to? This doesn't mean that you need a formal gown and a full face of makeup (I sometimes wear lipstick on a first date, though—it discourages the guy from going in for a kiss, which is convenient since I try to stand by the no-kissing-on-the-first-date rule), but it does mean that it's a good thing if they can tell that you dressed nicely for them.

My end goal is to look like a more polished version of myself.

I always ask for a general idea of what we will be doing so that I can pick the right clothing. I learned this rule after I was walking out the door to meet my date when he texted me to tell me to bring socks. It took me a second to decode this: He was taking me bowling. I was wearing a minidress and heels—so not the best choice! It's also kind of key to find out how tall he is so that you don't inadvertently tower over him (unless, of course, that's your thing).

The other X factor of date dressing revolves around the amount of skin to expose. Guys generally want to see your body, but that doesn't mean that they need to see the whole thing. Pick one part that you want to show off—whether it's your shoulders or your legs—and keep it demure elsewhere. You want to feel sexy—but comfortable. And I don't care what sort of justification you offer, but anything too tight or too short isn't sexy *or* comfortable!

Ultimately, I'm not above getting a guy's opinion. Girls view fashion in a very different way, which is why we love high-waisted pants and conceptual tops. Your friends might sign off on an outfit that would make an average guy scratch his head.

DAYTIME DATE

Even if your date is during the day you should still look nice. Just because you're meeting for coffee or a stroll in the park instead of dinner doesn't give you license to slack. If it's a sunny day and you're feeling girly, wear a flirty dress or skirt. Nice jeans and a pretty top will work if you want to keep it casual, but no sneakers with this option, please. Instead pair it with pretty flats, boots, or heels.

WEEKEND

The weekends are one of the few times in life when you should feel liberated to wear whatever you want. But, if you're anything like me, you might find that it's challenging to look relaxed without slipping into sloppy territory.

There is a big gray area between a put-together outfit . . . and sweatpants. I know it can be difficult after a long week of enduring cinched waists and uncomfortable heels, but fight the urge. Sweats were made to be worn inside your home, not to the supermarket, airport, or on late-night frozen-yogurt runs. You can be comfortable and look great; it just requires a little more effort. So stock up on easy pieces that don't take much thought (tanks, sundresses, casual T-shirts).

Small upgrades make a huge difference: Simple things like swapping your boring flip-flops for an embellished pair can instantly make an outfit more interesting. The weekends are also a great time to try a trend that you've been eyeing but don't feel comfortable wearing to work or school.

ONE LITTLE BLACK DRESS, FIVE WAYS

Here's an example of how one dress can be worn many ways— and how much accessories can influence your look.

BOHEMIAN: Vintage jean jacket, lace slip, sandals

EVENING: Embellished stilettos, great clutch, nice jewelry

PREPPY: Cardigan, pearls, Mary Jane heels

CASUAL: Oversized cardigan, ballet flats

EDGY: Leather jacket, gladiator ankle boots

STRATEGY GUIDE

MIXING PATTERNS

Whether it's stripes and plaids, or florals, paisleys, and polka dots, wearing two patterns at once can be surprisingly chic. There are a few things to keep in mind.

- Choose patterns that share a neutral background, like brown, black, white, or gray.

- Make sure that the patterns have at least a few colors in common: If you're mixing a navy stripe shirt with a floral print skirt, make sure that a similar blue is part of the floral print—this is important if the two items don't share the same neutral background (see the first point).

- Mix up the scale of the prints: a teeny-tiny polka dot with big, oversized stripes—or even stripes on stripes, so long as they're not the same size.

- Don't go overboard: Only two pieces in one outfit should have a pattern, and there should be at least one other element (a cardigan, tights, belt, or skirt) that's completely plain.

MIXING VINTAGE AND NEW

I love working vintage clothes and accessories into my wardrobe (see p. 47 for more on sourcing the good stuff), but it has to be kept in check. Try to limit yourself to one vintage piece per outfit (like the vintage shirt I pair with my black skirt), otherwise you run the risk of looking too era-specific, or like you basically raided your grandma's closet. This is even more true if you're wearing a major vintage piece like an evening gown or a day dress: If this is the case, skip the sequined cardigan or the fur stole. Instead, update the ensemble with an on-trend item like a cropped leather bomber, an oversized boyfriend blazer, or ankle booties. It's all about mixing it up: Surprising combinations tend to look fabulous and can make an otherwise dated garment look fresh.

For those of you who freak out at the idea of wearing someone else's discarded clothing, think about mixing in a few vintage accessories instead, whether it's a bejeweled necklace or a woven leather belt. (Full disclosure: I'm a little iffy on vintage shoes—it just seems kind of yucky.) It really is one of the best ways to add patina and texture to an outfit. And, if you're willing to hunt, buying vintage often costs a fraction of what you'll pay for a comparable item that's new.

HOW TO FIGURE OUT
THE PERFECT STYLE PROPORTION

The most important rule is to dress for balance. If you're wearing skinny jeans or something equally fitted below, pair them with a more voluminous top. Alternately, if you're working a drapey blouse, skip the baggy boyfriend jeans. Nobody looks good when their body is drowning in fabric, but an overly body-conscious, tight-all-over look isn't very flattering, either. (Leave a little to the imagination, ladies.)

When I'm getting dressed, I think about the part of my body that I'd most like to play up that day. If it's my legs, I put on my skinnies (they're kind of a uniform, to be honest)—and then usually add some variation of a slouchy tee or an oversized blazer. If I'm wearing a short dress, I make sure it's not too tight. (Again, showing a lot of legs is revealing enough.) But if I want to wear my volume on the bottom—full skirt, boyfriend jeans—then I make sure that I'm pairing it with a fitted tank or jacket. Really, it's a balancing act.

If there's a specific body issue that you're trying to dress around—whether it's an overly endowed chest or a boyish figure—turn to p. 111 where I address it all.

WHAT A TAILOR CAN DO FOR YOU

There's a misconception that everything we buy should fit flawlessly—but beyond the fact that nobody really has the body of a true fit model (the figure around which all the patterns are constructed), most of us aren't perfectly proportioned, either. (I'm definitely not—for more on this, see p. 109.) And the true irony is that at any photo shoot—whether it's for a magazine or a catalog—if you were to turn the fit model around and shoot her from the back, you'd see about fifty safety pins and thirty binder clips all over the item of clothing being modeled. This is the quickest and easiest on-site way to make something look tailor-made during a photo shoot without enlisting an actual tailor. (For more on what happens at photo shoots, see p. 213.)

There, I said it: A tailor. Sure, it's not necessarily cheap, but having someone customize your clothing for you is the fastest way to a bespoke fit. You can't exactly walk around with a back full of binder clips! Having someone take in and let out your clothing wherever necessary will do much more for flattering your figure than a hundred consecutive days at the gym.

HOW TO MAKE
THINGS FIT PERFECTLY,
ON THE FLY

If a garment doesn't need significant alterations, there are lots of minor tweaks you can make in seconds.

HEMMING: A light, quick, running stitch along the bottom of a dress or skirt that needs to be shortened is actually easy: no fashion degree or sewing machine required. Basic thread leaves no mark behind if you need to pull it out and start over—or if you ultimately decide to replace your handiwork with the real deal. (For tips on shortening your own jeans while preserving the original hem, turn to p. 25.) I also keep a bin of safety pins on hand, since sometimes you just need two or three of those to make short work of a simple hem (particularly if it's on a part of the garment that's not very visible). Alternately, double-sided hemming tape from a company like Bristols 6 accomplishes the same thing: I usually iron the crease first to give it extra staying power.

CUFFING: It's one of the simplest styling tricks out there, but a quick cuff—on a jacket, shirt, or pant leg—is an easy way to make a piece look a little edgier. It's also a great way to rein in extra volume (just roll the fabric under a bit before you cuff it) if something is swimming on you (like a men's button-down shirt). It doesn't need to be perfect or symmetrical. Often, I push my sleeves up my arms a bit after cuffing them, just to make it look a little more laid-back and undone.

BELTING: There is generally no better ally for a girl than a great belt, since the waist is invariably always good to highlight—nothing accomplishes this more effectively than a waist-cinching wrap. And in this age of the voluminous top, it's the best means for tackling all that extra fabric, too, which generally drowns a lot of girls' figures. A belt is also very handy for making a skirt that's a little too big work—I fold the waistband over a tiny bit, pin it, and then use the belt to conceal my handiwork.

PINNING: If a top is too big and you don't feel like using a belt to create a waistline, pull a handful of fabric together in the back, and pin it with a vintage broach. It takes about a second but is super chic. Just make sure that you're not going to need to sit all night because it can be a little uncomfortable to recline on jewelry.

HOW TO WEAR COLOR

It's a bummer that so many people are color shy, because it's one of the most appealing ways to make an outfit more interesting. Black is chic and all, but red is wayyyy more fun. If you're a bit reluctant, start with small doses (a shoe or a bag) and work yourself up to a brightly hued top. For the truly adventurous, consider layering variations of the same shade: like a mint-green top under a forest-green cardigan.

Sadly, there's no universal color chart that will tell you exactly what shades are most flattering for your skin tone. In fact, it changes all the time, from season to season. (There are lots of colors I can pull off when tan that I would never attempt in the dead of winter.) The quickest way to tell if something will work is to hold it up to your face under a fairly bright light to see what it does to your complexion. If there's no mirror handy, the general rule of thumb is that the deeper and more jewel-like the tone, the more wearable it becomes. Anything pastel or washed out can get dicey—fast.

And if your favorite color turns you pasty (for me, it's purple—which I love, despite the fact that it makes me look terrible), that doesn't mean that you can't wear it at all. Just don't wear it next to your face. Instead, opt for a skirt, pants, or even shoes in variations of that tone.

STYLE IS LAWLESS

Not to belabor the point and all, but it can't be said enough: There are no rules when it comes to fashion. You can wear white all winter (ivory-hued pants look great with riding boots and a big, oversized sweater), despite those old-fashioned types who say it should all be stashed after Labor Day. It's difficult to do, but black and navy can happily coexist in the same outfit. (You just need to mix up the textures—a navy blazer doesn't work that well with black work pants but definitely integrates nicely with black jeans.) Look around for good style inspiration, and you can make almost anything work.

BODY ISSUES

When you live in a city like Los Angeles, you're bound to encounter a ton of body dysmorphia: In fact, I have yet to meet a girl—starlets and models included—who is completely happy with her figure. This is pretty tragic, when you think about it, and a colossal waste of emotional energy. Listen: I will never love my thighs—it doesn't matter how much my weight may fluctuate, but my upper legs stay the same. (To me, they're short and wide.) But you've probably never singled out my thighs as overly well endowed, right? This could be because I'm the only one who notices. Think about this when you're turning the microscope on yourself. You can pick anything apart, which is why I always think it's the best policy to overlook those parts of your body that you don't love, in favor of playing up the parts of your body that you do. So I try to ignore my upper thighs, and show off my shoulders and collarbone instead.

THE FLATTERING POINTS ON ANY WOMAN'S BODY

This may sound a little crazy but stick with me here: There are a handful of points on every woman's figure that are almost universally delicate and feminine: the wrists, the ankles, and the collarbone. Making them visible, whether it's via a bracelet-sleeve jacket, a pair of cropped pants, or a V-neck top, is always flattering.

HOW TO SHOW OFF YOUR . . .

SHOULDERS AND ARMS: Strapless dresses instantly draw the eye to the upper arm and shoulder area. And any sort of halterlike top accomplishes the same thing. (If you're narrow up top, this will make you look a bit broader across the back.) I usually purchase tops one size larger so they drape off my shoulders and look more feminine.

LEGS: When it comes to skirt length, there's really no standard for a flattering cut. Some girls love their knees and like to reveal them—others would rather cover them with fabric. Just take your skirt and use your hands to lift and lower the hem to see what looks best. Also if you prefer a higher hemline but don't want to show too much skin, tights are always a great option.

Keep in mind that the fuller the skirt, the thinner your legs will appear—anything too tight will have the opposite affect. (The worst is the sausage-in-casing look.)

And you don't have to show a lot of skin to play up your legs: A pair of well-fitting skinny or straight-leg jeans accomplishes the same thing.

CLEAVAGE: There are a lot of things you can do to play up your cleavage without busting out a deeply plunging top and a push-up bra. Subtlety is really important here since anything overly revealing gives off a slightly trashy vibe. I think a good guideline is to never show more than three-quarters of an inch of shadow, which you can accomplish via a scoop-neck or V-neck T-shirt or sweater. Tip: If your top is loose *and* low-cut, make sure you're not flashing everyone when you bend over.

BUTT: Anything fitted through the butt and hips is a good choice, whether it's a knee-length pencil skirt or a great pair of black pants. The key is to make sure that you don't wear anything too volume-heavy, such as an A-line skirt or a pair of overly baggy pants, otherwise you'll just look large rather than curvy.

WAIST: Don't disguise your waist with a lot of fabric (such as a tentlike top). Instead, go for pieces that are tailored, like a collared shirt, or a T-shirt that's not too slouchy. As mentioned, a waist-cinching belt is a great way to draw attention to an hour-glass shape (or to create one from scratch). If you're wearing multiple layers, including a jacket, go for one that either nips in or is cut off right at the waist. Both are a great means for drawing the eye to this part of the body.

I started wearing makeup in the seventh grade. I had one of those crazy palettes with about seventy-two different eye shadow colors, which was pretty convenient since, back then, I liked to match my eyelids to my outfit. I used (and wore) an excessive amount of purple, a color that doesn't actually do me any favors; maybe this is why I don't wear eye shadow anymore! The kit also came with two "face" colors, with which I did a fair amount of experimenting. One was for skin much darker than mine, the other for skin much lighter. I tried the lighter shade, and it made me so pale that on one of our family Christmas cards I looked like a mime. Whenever I do anything awful, my mom threatens to post that picture on the internet.

Like everyone else I know, I basically taught myself how to do makeup—and created a lot of cringe-worthy photo moments in the process. You're bound to make a lot of mistakes, but that's an important part of the learning curve. With time and help (like from this chapter!), you'll figure out your own way to play up your best features, without looking like you have too much of a "face" on.

In addition to learning by trial and error, I've been lucky enough to work with a lot of talented makeup artists over the years, and have picked up tons of tips. (FYI, don't be shy about asking for tutorials at your local makeup counter—especially if you're willing to buy a product or two.) Amy Nadine Rosenberg is one of my all-time favorite makeup artists, and she helped me develop what I now think of as my signature look. I love Amy not only because of how she wields her makeup brushes but because she's always respectful of my comfort level. Like with eye shadow: However irrational my fear of it might be (I think it makes me look older and overly made-up), she never puts it on my face. We've all been coached to believe that every makeup component is essential for a "complete" look, but that's just not true. Read on, because Amy provides tons of tips for doing the looks I love best, at home.

BUT . . . before we get to the fun part, I need to insert a serious disclaimer about beauty. It's only skin-deep, right? Well, make sure you're taking care of your skin—even if your skin is too young to show signs of aging. As you probably know, I grew up in Orange County, where sunbathing is about as ingrained as teeth brushing. I basically lived on the beach, and when I wasn't on the beach, I was playing soccer or tennis outdoors. Unfortunately, I was never as diligent about sunscreen application as I should have been. I didn't burn very often so I didn't think that I needed to wear SPF everyday. You can imagine my surprise when the dermatologist told me—at the ripe old age of fourteen—that he would be removing precancerous cells from areas on my back. Even after visiting a plastic surgeon post-surgery, I still have the scars today. So slather up, even if it's not particularly "sunny" outside, or you think your skin tans so easily that you never burn. Those UV rays are a serious threat to your health, and I bear the battle wounds to prove it!

DAYTIME LOOK

"The goal here is to create a look that is pretty and effortless—
direct sunlight has a way of revealing makeup, so keep it light and low-key!"—Amy Nadine

FACE

After you've washed, toned, and applied day cream to your face (with SPF!), follow these steps:

1. Warm up a dab of sheer foundation or tinted moisturizer in the palm of your hand, just enough that it's undetectable. (Don't stress about blemishes. Those will be addressed later.)

2. Do a quick sweep all over your face *and* neck with a foundation brush or, believe it or not, your fingers. (Fingertips are the best means for conquering hard-to-reach areas, just be sure to wash them first.) If you protect your face with sunblock and a hat, your shoulders and face

may not be the same color. Match the foundation to your chest, or else your face will be dramatically paler than your body (which for anyone in my line of work can be a red-carpet *disaster*).

3. Dab concealer on any problem areas and blend it in. Using a concealer that's an exact match in color can correct problems like under-eye circles, blemishes, or broken capillaries (see p. 138 if you have more questions about this).

4. Dust some translucent loose powder along the forehead, nose, and chin, leaving cheeks untouched.

BLUSH AND BRONZING

While lots of blush colors work well on most people, one that is apricot or peachy colored is a good, basic standby—and if there's a range, go for one that's slightly more orange in shade. Otherwise, it will turn pink once it's on the face. Cream blush is pretty, but it's high-maintenance, since it absorbs into the skin and requires reapplication. So choose a matte, powder blush for day. Smile at yourself in the mirror, and sweep some onto the apples of your cheeks to create a pretty, "flushed" effect. Then dust some translucent powder over it to set it in place.

For the California Girl glow, bronzing is key. Buy a matte, non-orange bronzing powder (it should look light brown or dark taupe) and a kabuki-style brush, which is key for mimicking a natural tan. Then follow these simple steps:

1. While looking in the mirror, suck in your cheeks.

2. Sweep the bronzer across the hollows of your cheeks and directly below and on top of your cheekbones, starting on the outside of your apples and following the bone all the way to your ears.

3. Dab some bronzer on your temples, hairline, along the sides of your nose, and under your jawline in light, circular motions.

4. Brush your neck with bronzer, too, so there's not a line between neck and face.

5. To make it "real" looking, blend it well by using the same brush with a tiny bit of translucent powder on it—swirl it back over the areas until there are no lines between the bronzed and un-bronzed skin.

EYES

"There's no love lost when it comes to Lauren and eye shadow. But there are other ways to accentuate your eyes."—Amy Nadine

You can create high drama by defining your eyes with black liquid liner—it has a reputation for being tricky, but it's much easier than it seems:

1. Rest your elbow on something sturdy like a bathroom counter so that you only need to move your wrist (controlling the movement of your hand is the trick to mastering liquid eyeliner).

MASTERING FAKE EYELASHES

False eyelashes sound terrifying and complicated but putting them on is actually pretty easy once you get the hang of it—and they add instant glamour. I wanted no part of putting them on myself, until Amy convinced me I could do it, too. Though individual lashes are harder to control (they can flip on their side while the glue is setting), and they have to be placed one by one, the final effect is natural-looking and exceptionally flattering. Strip lashes work, too, but they're a bit more obvious.

At your local drugstore, pick up individual sets of Short, Medium, Long, and Mini flare lashes. If you order a combo pack online, make sure you buy an extra set of Minis. You'll also need lash glue—glues that dry clear are best. If you're comfortable with using your fingers, go for it (it gives extra control), though most makeup artists prefer to use tweezers. It's totally a matter of personal preference.

1. Apply two coats of mascara on your top and bottom lashes.

2. Place a small dollop of lash glue onto the back of the hand. Let it dry for at least a minute so it gets nice and tacky.

3. With tweezers or your fingers, pull out three Longs, four Mediums, three Shorts,

and three Minis, and place them in separate rows on the back of your hand. (This is per eye.)

4. Starting with the outside corner of one eye, place two Longs on the very end, as close to each other as possible. Point them outward and at a 45-degree angle to get a cat-eye look.

5. Directly next to the two Longs, start adding lashes, moving toward the center of your eye in this order: one Medium, one Long, three Mediums, and then three Shorts. If you don't have a lot of space between your lash line and your eyebrow and the Longs look too costumey, swap them out for Mediums (five Mediums and five Shorts).

6. On your bottom lash line place three Minis on the outside corners, carefully inserting them in between the real lashes. If your own lashes are super long, use three Shorts instead. Just make sure that you apply them so that they're pointing down and not up (invert them).

PERFECT MAKEUP IN LESS THAN FIVE MINUTES

"Some things are good in small doses: Too much makeup can sometimes make you look too 'done,' particularly if you're doing nothing more than running around town for the afternoon." —Amy Nadine

Amy Nadine has trained me well. Now I can look great in six easy steps:

1. Using a sponge, apply a powder-foundation formula (a cream base that turns into a powder). It's simple to use and because it provides great coverage, you can skip the concealer and powder. You can literally "wipe" it on your face and neck. (30 seconds)

2. Apply blush to the apples of your cheeks and bronzer to your hairline, temples, cheekbones, nose, chin, and neck. (60 seconds)

3. Line your eyes with a kohl pencil or wet eye shadow. (60 seconds)

4. Apply mascara. (60 seconds)

5. Slick on your favorite lipstick or gloss. (10 seconds)

6. With your 80 seconds to spare, either add one pretty wash of color to your entire eyelid and crease before you apply the liner (this doesn't work for me but looks great on my friends!), fill in your brows, or quickly spot-conceal.

HOW TO GO FROM DAY TO NIGHT IN LESS THAN 10 MINUTES

You don't have to start your makeup from scratch when you're heading straight from the office to an event, or from school to a party. These key steps will transform your face:

1. Assess your makeup. If it's cakey, mist your face with a refreshing toner and smooth out any creases with a wet sponge. If the foundation is gone, reapply a powder-foundation formula with a sponge. (60 seconds)

2. Reapply bronzer and blush with a slightly heavier hand. Add a highlighting powder just above the cheekbones. (60 seconds)

3. Add a wash of color to your eyelid—it can be consistent across the lid, or you can do a darker shade in the crease. If it's the latter approach, blend with your fingertip. (60 seconds)

4. Redo the eyeliner and make it thicker and/or elongated. Apply liner to the bottom lash line and on the water line. (60 seconds)

5. Put on another coat of mascara. (60 seconds)

6. Optional: Add some false eyelashes. (180 seconds)

7. Slick on a nude, light pink, or peach lipstick and gloss. (60 seconds)

CHAPTER EIGHT
Hair

*J*ust like with fashion, there are major hair trends: One season every girl on the runway will sport a pixie-ish bob; during another, it's long, saltwater-kissed waves. I've done my share of hair experimenting—in high school I dyed mine maroon, red, brown, and even bleached it, and a few years ago I attempted a bob, which looked less chic and more soccer mom. But after those few minor lapses in judgment, I pretty much decided to stick with what works best for me: long, blond hair, styled with a loose curl. I justify this with a simple argument: Yes, hair grows—but it grows slooooowly!

Sure, there have been times when I've desperately wanted a different look. But wise hair stylists have pointed out to me that what I'm craving, whether it's perfect ringlets or sleek, black straight hair, is not attainable with scissors, since what I'm asking for is completely different hair. Much like with your figure, it's best to play up what you already have than try to override what nature gave you.

If you're dead set on a transformation, try it out first. You wouldn't buy a car without test-driving it, so do a little research before doing something irreversible. If you want a new hair color, march yourself down to the closest wig store (not a cheesy Halloween store, a nice wig store) and try on as many as you can. I've saved myself from some near disasters this way. You can also use color drops, which you apply to dry strands, to check different shades. (The color washes out in the shower.) The drops won't lighten your hair, though. If you're gunning for length, clip in some extensions before you go to the trouble of growing it out, and if you want something shorter, pin your hair up into a faux-bob first.

I first met Christine Symonds when she was working at the Warren-Tricomi Salon in Los Angeles, and while I'd always had a pretty good handle on styling my own hair, when she got her hands on my head it was eye-opening. She was great about listening to what I wanted, which is sometimes a difficult quality to find in a stylist. When I became obsessed with goddess braids and twists, she found countless ways to incorporate them into my hairstyle, ultimately turning my otherwise relatively unremarkable hair into my favorite outfit accessory of all. She also helped me get healthier locks. One of the pitfalls of maintaining longer strands is that the ends get dry: If you stop to think about it, those final inches have been on my head for a long time, and they've had many intimate moments with heat-based styling tools and other damaging factors. This is why it's become extremely important for me to learn how to take care of my hair; having it processed and styled constantly really takes a toll.

Since Christine is pretty much my hair guru, I wanted to impart her wisdom to you, too. I'm also sharing some at-home hair color wisdom I got from another one of my hair-stylists, Kristin Ess. She knows exactly how to pinpoint that perfectly natural shade. So read on for advice on making the most of what you have.

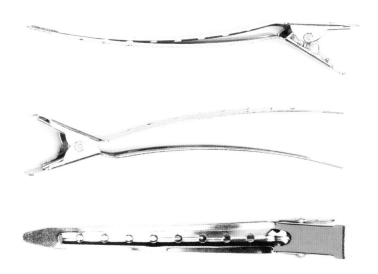

MAKING YOUR HAIR
WORK FOR YOU

"No matter how well you style your hair, the most important thing is its health. Damaged hair is never going to look like the luxurious locks in a shampoo commercial." —Christine Symonds

Besides the years of training and practice that your stylist has on you, that post-salon "wow" factor is also due to having a set of unhindered hands—and eyes—on all parts of your head. Quite frankly, it's tough to do your own hair. But despite these limitations, you can get pretty close.

First and foremost, you have to keep your hair healthy—it's difficult to smooth and control dried-out strands and frayed ends. Invest in a good cut and quality products that are catered to your specific hair type, and splurge on a deep-conditioning treatment once a month. This adds a ton of shine! (If you don't want to go to the salon, there are hydrating hair masks you can buy at any beauty store that will do the trick at home.)

When you sit down in your stylist's chair, be realistic about the haircut you can handle. If you want to take a shower and walk out the door ten minutes later, certain styles just aren't for you.

WORKING WITH CURLY HAIR

Curly hair is fragile and prone to dryness, so make sure you're keeping it super moisturized. If it gets too brittle, it will become extra-prone to breakage. Invest in a light and hydrating conditioner.

- Ask your hairstylist to cut long layers into the curls—this will add a little volume. Just make sure the stylist doesn't go crazy, since you don't want a triangular-shaped head of hair.

- Let your hair air-dry (leave yourself plenty of time in the morning) and keep your hands away from it until it's dry to avoid creating frizz. Once 90 percent of the moisture is gone, you can style and play with it all you want.

MASTERING THE PERFECT WAVES (AND MAKING THEM LAST!)

The idea here is to make your hair look like it is naturally full of body, so don't worry if the curls aren't perfectly symmetrical.

- Apply a volumizing or texturizing mousse to freshly washed hair.

- Using a towel, roughly dry your hair—flip your head upside down and rub vigorously to create some lift at the roots.

- Once your hair is completely dry, using a 1"-1.5" curling iron (anything smaller will create ringlets), wrap medium sections of hair around the barrel away from your face. This doesn't have to be perfect—you can choose sections at random—but make sure to get all of your hair.

- Comb your fingers through the waves to break up the curls a little bit, and finish with a light-hold hair spray.

- At night, put your hair in two loose, low buns when you sleep. Twist the hair toward the center of the head to maintain the direction of the curl.

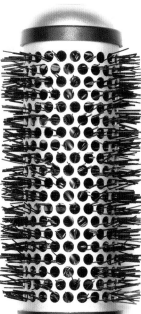

A STEP-BY-STEP GUIDE TO THE BEST AT-HOME BLOW-OUT

It can take some time to master this, so practice, practice, practice! In the interim, invest in a good flatiron to smooth out your hair afterward, if you can't get it perfectly sleek immediately.

- Divide your hair into three sections, two at the base of the neck, and one rectangular section up top: Clip up the hair that you're not working on so that it stays out of the way. If you have a cowlick, attack it immediately, so that you can control it before it starts to dry. Otherwise, start at one of the sections at the base of the neck.

- Aim the blow-dryer in the same direction the hair grows to minimize frizz. Most dryers come with an attachment called a nozzle, which streamlines the hot air and directs it through a small opening at the end. This is very important to use if your hair is difficult to manage.

- Once you reach the top of your head, grab a medium-sized round brush and blow-dry the pieces back and away from the face. This creates lift at the roots—and those perfect swept-back-looking pieces around the face.

- If your hair is super fine, take four large Velcro rollers and position them in a row across the top of the head. Just make sure to wrap the hair away from your face.

- If you have fringe, leave your bangs for last and switch to a flat brush—you don't want any extra volume here!

SPECIAL OCCASION HAIR

It may be counterintuitive, but don't spend too much time fiddling with your hair before a big event—less is always more. The look should be natural, soft, and *touchable* (easy on the hair spray!) so that you feel like a slightly fancier version of yourself. Overdo it and it will look more like bad prom/bridesmaid hair—or worse, a helmet.

SIMPLE UNDONE UPDO

Undone elegance at its best!

- Follow the steps above to create some waves—you want extra texture in your hair for this look to hold. There's no need to curl your entire head: Focus instead on the pieces around your face and the top section of hair.

- Using the line from your forehead to the base of your neck as a guide, divide your hair into three vertical sections. Leaving the two side sections alone, gather all the hair in the middle section and pull it into a low, loose bun. Fasten it with a clear hair tie. Taking random pieces of the bun, bobby pin them into a low, wide shape. Think of it as though you are mirroring the shape of your hairline.

- Incorporate the sides bit by bit, loosely pinning small sections into the bun.

- Let any short layers around your face fall naturally.

- Spray lightly with hair spray.

SLEEK PONYTAIL

This is a great, super-modern nighttime look.

- Prep already dry, straight hair with a polish to tame any flyaways.

- Figure out your part: One in the center will make the look a bit bolder, but a side part works well, too. You can also forgo one altogether.

- Gather your hair in one hand and position the bundle at the occipital bone, which is where the back of your head starts to curve down.

- With your free hand, use a boar-bristle brush to smooth all the hair into the ponytail.

- Using a metal-free hair tie, secure the ponytail (the smaller the band, the better).

- Take a small strand of hair and wrap it around the elastic for a more polished look; use a bobby pin that's the same shade as your hair to fix the end down.

Hint: For a day-friendly version of this look, keep it all a bit more tousled. Instead of using a brush to smooth the hair, use your fingers to create a beachy vibe.

EXECUTING THE GODDESS BRAID

Full disclosure: The first time I wore a side braid, it was to hide an unfortunate self-bangs-cutting incident. But then I ended up loving the way it looked. If you're feeling bored with your hair, adding a braid or twist can make a simple hairstyle more interesting.

- Apply a finishing cream to hair to tame any flyaways. (Avoid serums since they can make hair look greasy.)

- Gather a one- to two-inch section of hair (depending on the thickness of the strands) and braid to the desired length.

- Secure it to your head with bobby pins that match your hair color—I like Scunci's "no slip grip" ones.

- Spray with a light-hold hair spray.

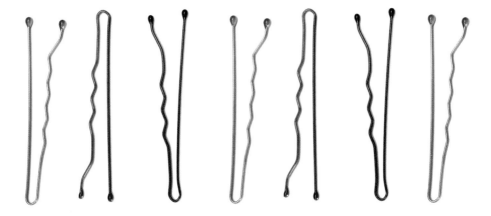

WORKING HAIR ACCESSORIES INTO YOUR LOOK

Adding vintage clips, leather cord, and even simple headbands is the perfect way to play up your hair with a minimal investment of time and effort.

HEADBANDS: This is a great go-to if you want to keep your hair out of your face, especially if you're attempting to make it last for two days in a row. Make sure that the headband sits forward on your head. It should be only an inch and a half from your hairline.

LEATHER CORD: Either a strand of suede or even fun ribbons are a great way to get a bohemian vibe (an antique necklace works, too). Tie it around your head so that it runs across your forehead. Be sure to choose something dainty: the larger the piece, the more attention it draws.

HAIR CLIPS: Search out big antique earrings or broaches at the local flea market and superglue them to barrette backs. Clip on the side of a bun for instant glamour, or leave hair down and pin up one side for a retro-inspired look.

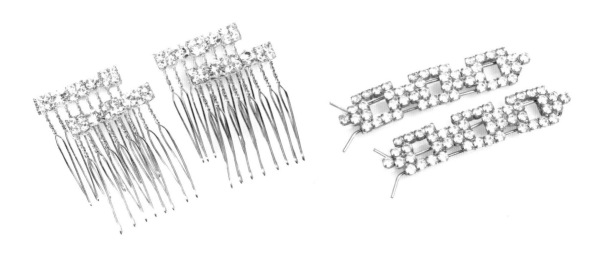

HOW TO MAKE YOUR HAIR LAST BETWEEN WASHES

Ideally, you should wash your hair every other day, though this can vary wildly depending on what kind of hair you have. Try to be consistent: Your scalp will produce an appropriate amount of oil once it knows what to expect. (In fact, it will eventually self-clean if you leave your hair for long enough, though I don't recommend testing this out! It's a little gross.)

- Invest in a high-quality dry shampoo. Spray on your roots, let it sit for a few minutes, and then brush the powder through. These dry shampoos smell great and go a long way toward controlling grease.

- Keep your hands out of your hair! The more you touch, the more you're likely to stimulate your scalp. Also, there's plenty of oil and dirt on your fingertips, which you're essentially donating to your hair.

- Save the conditioner for your ends, which need the most moisturizing. Often it's too heavy on the roots anyway and will make it more difficult to style hair.

GETTING HAIR COLOR RIGHT

"Changing your hair color should be fun." —Kristin Ess

There are lots of options when it comes to getting your hair dyed, from single process (the same shade all over, without any highlights), to lowlights (when darker pieces are added into the mix), to toner, which is essentially just a gloss. The most important thing is to find a colorist who you have complete confidence in. (It can be difficult and costly to correct bad dye jobs.) Essentially, you need your equivalent of my Kristin Ess. As mentioned, I strongly recommend going to a wig store first to rule out shades that will absolutely not work with your complexion and then trust your pro to find a good, flattering tone. Any reference materials like pictures from magazines are good to bring along so your colorist can get a clear idea of exactly what you like. (It can be better than words, since those can involve a lot of -ishes and -esques . . . you know, like a strawberry-blond-ish auburnesque color that's not too red!)

DYEING YOUR HAIR AT HOME

If your hair is a very basic color, and you're not interested in the complexity of highlights and lowlights, it's safe to do a temporary color gloss or glaze at home. This isn't a bad move, too, if you're trying to extend the time between trips to your colorist, since they can keep hair vibrant and shiny for not a lot of cash. Look for colors on the shelf that are labeled "gloss," "glaze," or "wash out within four weeks." These tend to be the subtlest, and thus the easiest to use—plus, they usually don't have any peroxide or ammonia so they'll eventually rinse out.

CARING FOR
COLOR-TREATED HAIR

Every time you shampoo your hair, you're stripping a little bit of color out of the strand—this can be helpful if you went too dark, but if you'd like to prolong the life of your treatment, try to wash your hair only every other day. Products created specifically for colored hair are also a good investment, since they can actually add color back into the hair.

Quick Tip: Controlling Static

This becomes a particularly annoying problem in winter, when the air is dry and crackly. Plus, warm woolly hats and winter jackets don't help! There are a few things you can do to minimize flyaways.

- Gently rub a dryer sheet over your head. It sounds crazy, but they smell great and they keep static in check.

- Spray a product like Static-Cling into all of your hats and any other pieces of clothing that cause static.

WORK

THE FOOLPROOF INTERVIEW OUTFIT

The right interview attire requires a lot of thought. The basic underlying principle should be to dress as though your mother picked out your outfit, so long as your mother is one of those people who tried to swipe you with a lint brush as you were walking out the door.

You don't have to bury your entire sense of style—after all, potential employers are looking for clues about and insights into your personality—but limit the "flair" factor to your accessories. These should be relatively simple, too.

Aim for pieces that are tailored, well fitting, and appropriate (not sloppy, not tight, and not short). Tights and a cardigan are generally good additions, too, if you want your outfit to feel more layered and covered up.

And finally, look over your outfit the night before: Make sure it's rip- and stain-free, and that it doesn't need to be steamed. It's seriously uncomfortable to come to the realization that there's a big salad dressing stain on your pants when you're standing in the lobby!

DRESSING FOR THE JOB

Depending on what industry you're in, your work wardrobe might not be the most exciting segment of your closet. And this is okay. Focus instead on work essentials—blazers, button-downs, black pants—that fit really well. If they're perfectly tailored, you'll be much more inclined to wear them outside of the office, too. Often, because it's the least thrilling thing to spend money on, women choose ill-fitting, overly frumpy office attire. It doesn't have to be that way! Don't settle!

And despite the monochromatic palette and anti-fashion-forward silhouettes, you don't have to leave your personality at home. You just have to be subtle about it. A beautifully patterned silk scarf, a thin black patent belt, a colorful cashmere cardigan, a tasteful, yet statement-making

Cute Commuter Shoes for Working Girl Moments

I'd never support a panty-hose-and-white-tennis-shoe fashion moment, but I'm all for easing the commute—whether it's on foot, by subway, or behind the wheel of a car—with comfortable shoes. I used to walk two miles to and from class when I attended art school in San Francisco. The fact that San Francisco is basically made up of hills and that I had to haul about fifteen pounds of art equipment back and forth made heels out of the question. So I began to stockpile thin ballet flats, which I could easily toss into any of my handbags. They're perfect, because they don't look out of place in the elevator, or during those first few minutes when you're getting settled at your desk before you swap out your shoes (or one block away from school, where I stopped to change mine on the sidewalk). Most importantly: Don't toss the fabric bags that come with fancy heels—they're very handy for storing shoes during the commute. (You don't want them floating around your bag!)

necklace—all are easy ways to make an otherwise straightforward outfit a little bit more interesting.

WORK-TO-PARTY ATTIRE

I know a lot of women who store a few pairs of shoes at the office or in the trunk of their car. This is for easy swaps in case of blisters and also for when there's no time to go home before dinner or a party post-work. (A brightly colored pair of pumps can transform an entire outfit.) If I had an office job, I'd also store a small evening clutch in my desk and a handful of costume jewelry.

When an event calls for more than a minor shift in the dress code, work it into the outfit in the morning. A dress with a pair of opaque tights and Mary Janes is easy to shift from day to night. Lose the tights and sweater and add some peep-toes and a cute bag and you have a completely different look.

THINGS YOU SHOULD NEVER, EVER WEAR TO WORK

There are several parts of the body that should never see the inside of the office: your upper back, your lower back, your cleavage, and your toes. This roughly translates to no strapless tops, no halter tops, no strapless dresses, no low-cut blouses, no low-cut pants, and no flip-flops.

SCHOOL

FASHION VICTIM VS. FASHION PIONEER

The thing that breaks my heart the most about school is the overwhelming—yet unspoken—pressure to dress like everyone else. Caving is understandable, not only because it's nice to fit in (a form of camouflage, right?) but also because nobody wants to unwittingly become the butt of some mean girl's joke thanks to a "strange" outfit. Now, I know I don't have to live through it again with you, but all I can say is that giving in and floating downstream with that main current is the more tragic course. Real fashion victim territory! In high school my friends and I dressed so similarly, it looked like we had developed an actual uniform: same shoes, same jeans, same belt, same top. Sure, our denim washes and shirt colors may have varied, but that was as far as we strayed. If I could do it over, this would be my motto: Be brave and be different. Creating your own personal style is tricky and challenging—there will be days when you'll absolutely hate what you're wearing and want to run home for a do-over, but these are necessary steps for true mastery!

WORKING WITH A SCHOOL UNIFORM

There are lots of inspired ways to modify a standard school uniform. (Not to sound like your mom or anything, but there are plenty of ways without, um, making the skirt shorter.) If the uniform includes some sort of blazer or jacket, mine the local thrift stores for unusual badges and cool pins and decorate the lapels. If the jacket is cut baggy in the arms, roll the sleeves. And check the school policy on scarves and hair accessories: A brightly patterned scarf or headband, whether silk or cotton, is a great way to add some shots of color, and I love working vintage barrettes into any look. If the dress code is strict, you might have to get creative, but remember: You're doing it in the name of fashion.

Beyond stores like Forever 21 and H&M, where a bulk of the costume jewelry doesn't top $15, be sure to check your city for wholesale spots that are open to the public. (Alltherageonline.com, which you can shop online, has a huge store in New York City, for example.) This is where all the trendy boutiques stock up on necklaces and bracelets. If you go straight to the source, you're likely to save at least 50 percent. And don't overlook import stores: You can snap up an armful of Indian bangles for about $10, chandelier earrings for $20, and strands of African trade beads for as little as $5.

CHAPTER TEN
Travel

I have a love/hate relationship with my suitcase. I love my suitcase when I am filling (i.e., over-stuffing) it with lovely clothing options for fun occasions: a chiffon sundress to be worn exploring the vineyards and small towns of Italy, a sheer printed cover-up for layering over a bright bikini in Cabo San Lucas, or a tailored coat and brown leather boots intended for a fantastic dinner in a chic New York City restaurant. Then, there are those times when I absolutely hate it: the last-minute work trips that consist of red-eye flights, minimal sleep, and forking over favorite beauty products at airport security because they exceed the three-ounce limit (the collateral damage of attempting to travel with only a carry-on).

Dressing stylishly while on the road involves creating outfits from a small array of pieces, which is when accessorizing and styling tricks really come in handy. The idea is to bring a few key pieces to create the illusion of an entire wardrobe, and it is best if those items take up very little space. You can make the same button-down shirt work with jeans and boots for day that you can then wear tucked into a pencil skirt with heels for a nice dinner at night. And it's fun to figure this all out. Just make sure the outfits work before you get on the plane! Vacation is not the ideal time to test-drive a brand-new dress.

STRATEGIC PACKING

There are lots of variables to packing for a trip—where you're going, for how long, what you're doing when you get there, how you get there—but no matter the destination or purpose, the one constant of traveling in style is packing smartly.

There are two types of extreme packers: Those who bring their entire closet for a weekend getaway, and those who can assemble fourteen days' worth of outfits in Paris using only the contents of a carry-on. Everybody wants to be the master of the second scenario: Not only do you get to skip the baggage claim, but it's actually much easier to get dressed when you've thought it through beforehand and pared it down to the essentials. Plus, then you get to spend the first hour of your vacation enjoying the vacation rather than unpacking. And you get to pass the rest of your time just enjoying your trip, instead of sifting through your suitcase, figuring out what to wear.

Now I'm not a total minimalist: I will always bring more than I need (insurance!). But after years of traveling I've become a decent packer, which wasn't always the case. I learned the hard way how important it is to make a list before opening up the suitcase and throwing things in. One memorable example was the time I went on a beach vacation with my family when I was eleven years old. Being the procrastinator that I am, I left packing to the last minute and ended up shoving clothes into my suitcase in a mindless frenzy. The result: an oversized baggage charge (who knew summer dresses were so heavy? . . . I only packed fifteen!) and *not one* bathing suit to show for it. We were in a pretty remote spot, too, and the nearest gift shop only sold leopard-print one-pieces for a different generation. I spent my vacation running along the shore in shorts and oversized T-shirts.

As much as I would like to say I've grown up and changed my ways, I arrived in Miami not too long ago only to realize I didn't pack a single pair of shoes. (Some things never change.) But while I haven't perfected the process, I have improved my packing strategy quite a bit. A few days before takeoff, I jot down a quick list of activities and events (my itinerary, if you will), along with the key pieces required for each. On one long trip to Paris I actually planned my outfit for every day and photographed them. If you have the time to do this it's great because it pretty much takes all the stress out of the process.

Once I've narrowed down my options, I make sure that everything is clean (i.e., a dress for a red-carpet event, or my favorite skinny jeans for the plane) and easy to find (I once turned my entire apartment upside down the night before a flight looking for a pair of shoes that were at the cobbler's for a resoling). After I've outlined my outfits (with as much overlap of basic items as possible), I leave it alone until the night before, at which point it only takes about fifteen minutes to get my bag together.

MAXIMIZING SUITCASE SPACE

There are a few techniques for cramming as much as humanly possible into a bag. I find that rolling my clothing works best, not only to save space but also as a means for keeping it all relatively wrinkle-free. Shoes should be separated from each other (other-wise they take up too much room), and small items like socks and underwear should always be added last (they can slot into extra pockets of air—you can even stuff some of your socks into your shoes). To keep my necklaces from getting tangled, I roll them in washcloths; you can also store them in Ziploc bags (seal the chain at the halfway point so they don't tangle).

- 1 white oversized button-down (great cover-up once you've had too much sun, and cute when tied at the waist or tucked into a full skirt and belted)
- 1 tunic (when it's not on you at the beach, great with jeans at night)
- 1 daytime dress (ideally something that you can throw on over a bathing suit)
- 1 evening dress (black or neutral is best, so that you can re-accessorize it and wear it multiple nights)
- jewelry (something colorful and tropical is a good choice)
- 1-2 vintage belts (for the tunic, the dresses, and the full skirt)
- canvas carry-on tote (that can double as a beach bag during the day)
- 1 clutch for evening (if you really want to save space, use this as your wallet as well)
- 1 pair of jeans (for the flight and chilly nights)
- 1 blazer (if during the winter months, it can work as a light jacket to and from the airport, and an extra layer in the evening hours)
- undergarments (and maybe a tank top with a built-in bra for those times when you get too much sun—try not to!)

WORK TRIP (THREE DAYS)

Create a capsule wardrobe by keeping everything monochromatic—and don't stress too much. If something comes up and your trip is extended, you'll likely be able to buy what you need while on the road. Chances are, you'll be in a well-supplied city.

- 1 light trench coat (khaki, navy, or black; ideally it is also waterproof, though if you hit rain, there's probably an umbrella stand nearby)
- 1 blazer (black or navy, which can also work as a light jacket)

- 1 pair of black pants (well fitting and hemmed to work with flats)
- 2 work shirts (white always looks crispest)
- 1 pencil skirt (black, gray, or navy)
- 1 cashmere cardigan (black or navy)
- 1 pair of opaque tights (black)
- 1 pair of high heels (black)
- 1 pair of flats (black)
- 2 T-shirts
- 1 pair of comfortable walking flats (can be a sneaker or something slightly fancier)
- 1 pair of jeans (for non-work dinners with friends)
- 2 scarves (to pull off the same outfit twice!)
- 1 black tote (spacious enough to serve as a carry-on)
- jewelry
- undergarments

CITY VACATION (FIVE DAYS)

Pack shoes that you know are comfortable because you'll likely be on your feet all day. (The sidewalks of a major city are not the place to break in previously unworn flats.) And go heavier on tops than bottoms (2:1 ratio); blouses and T-shirts take up less space, and you can wear the same pair of jeans every day and nobody will know the difference.

- 2 pairs of jeans (one should be in a clean, basic wash so you can wear them out at night)
- 3 evening/party tops (which can also work during the day)

- 1 nice blouse (for daytime)
- 3 T-shirts
- 1 cardigan (cut slightly long)
- 1 blazer or cropped jacket (crisp but easy to move in)
- 1 dress (for going to dinner or out at night)
- 2 scarves (for warmth and splashes of color)
- 2 pairs of flats (colorful and comfortable)
- 1 pair of heels (for evening)
- 1 pair of sneakers (just in case)
- 1 lightweight satchel (you need to be able to carry this for hours—it may sound crazy, but consider a leather backpack as another good option)
- jewelry
- undergarments

Make Room for Shopping

I travel to New York a lot for work, and time and time again I find myself with the same dilemma. I arrive with a bag stuffed to the brim and then . . . I shop. One time I actually had to buy a new suitcase in New York to get all my clothes home. So if you're headed to a shopping destination, leave extra room in your bag. Or find an American Apparel store and snap up a cheap, nylon tote.

WEEKEND GETAWAY TO
SOMEWHERE WARM

Depending on where you live, you might have a favorite quick escape—mine are usually to Vegas.

- 2 party dresses (you can't wear the same thing twice)
- 1 pair of going-out shoes (these should be comfortable, since your nights will likely be long—and involve dancing!)
- 1 bathing suit
- 1 sundress (to wear during the days—it should be a basic color, like black or white, so you can camouflage it with different accessories)
- 1 big hat (optional—these can be a pain to travel with)
- 1 pair of sunglasses
- 1 pair of flip-flops
- 1 cotton scarf
- 2 necklaces
- 1 pair of flats (for your abused feet the day after a big night)
- 1 pair of jeans
- 2 cute tops
- 1 pair of pajamas (for sleeping in until noon and ordering room service in comfort!)
- undergarments (Spanx are optional, but a good idea if you're wearing a dress that's body-conscious)

- 1 pair of boots (warm and winterproof—it's best if they're not too precious since you'll be exposing them to snow and salt)
- 1 pair of jeans
- 2 T-shirts
- 1 thermal top (to layer underneath T-shirts)
- 1 pair of comfortable, stretchy athletic pants (for putting on after any cold-weather activities)
- 2 blouses
- 1 cashmere sweater (for extra warmth)
- 1 down vest
- 1 winter coat
- 1 woolly hat
- 1 scarf
- 1 pair of gloves
- undergarments (including warm socks and long underwear)

CHAPTER ELEVEN

Events and Parties

DECODING THE INVITATION

I've received a lot of invitations over the years, complete with head-scratching dress codes. Smart casual? What does that even mean? This sort of unclear directive can be frustrating, since I think you owe it to your guests to take some of the guesswork out of it! Regardless, the best rule of thumb is: When in doubt, shoot for being overdressed.

Here are some general guidelines:

CASUAL: Anything goes. (Almost . . . try to put in a little effort.)

SMART OR BUSINESS CASUAL: Skirt or nice pants, with a proper blouse or top. (Some say that you can wear jeans to a "smart casual" event, so long as the other elements are slightly more dressed up, but I would play it safe and skip them altogether.)

COCKTAIL: A dress, plain and simple. It can be knee-length.

BLACK-TIE OPTIONAL: This is more of a distinction for guys than for girls. (It's the difference between a suit and a tux.) If it's black-tie optional, you can wear a fancy dress of any length.

BLACK-TIE: People say that black-tie always means floor length, but I disagree. So long as you're wearing something polished—with beautiful accessories—you can pull off a cocktail-length dress. It should feel distinctly evening-worthy (i.e., you would never wear it to a daytime event) to make the cut.

- Lift your arms ever so slightly away from your sides to engage the muscle—you want to show some differentiation between your arm and your side, too, so that it doesn't look like one big mass.

- If you're in a group shot and you're the tallest or largest, try to be in the middle, or at least in a position where you're flanked by two people—those on the end get the bum rap and will always appear bigger than they actually are.

- Study celebrity photographs—it's our job to know how to hold ourselves to show our best selves. (And honestly, after five years of being on camera, it's instinctual for me at this point.) You can pick up tons of pointers just by mimicking a pose that looks relaxed and happy. Here are a few of me to get you started:

THINGS TO AVOID WHEN
YOU'RE GETTING YOUR PICTURE TAKEN

Clothing with small patterns make video cameras go nuts (the screen will literally shimmer, and not in a good way)—plus, it tends to make the body look bigger. Bright colors photograph well and help mitigate the fact that the flash will wash you out. White is really tough—not only does it often end up looking transparent thanks to backlighting and flash, but it reflects a ton of light, which just makes you look bigger. (Darker colors have the opposite effect, since they absorb the light.) If you're being photographed from the waist up, don't wear too much volume up top (you don't have the benefit of whatever you're wearing below to balance out the outfit), and skip anything strapless, since it will make you look naked.

WHAT REALLY HAPPENS AT PHOTO SHOOTS—
PLUS, WHAT HAPPENS AFTER!

One last thing about pictures . . . It's great to take tips from pictures you see in magazines—I'm always using them for styling and makeup ideas. But please keep in mind that these are highly processed shots!

Remember what I said about people whose features are naturally photogenic? It pretty much has nothing to do with how beautiful they may or may not be in real life. In fact, this is why it's still essential to do screen tests in Hollywood—as gorgeous as someone may be, you just can't tell whose face will read well on film.

So, beyond the physical structure already at play, when you have your picture taken for a magazine, there's a veritable crew of people on-set to make sure that you look amazing: makeup artists, hairstylists, manicurists, tailors, stylists, plus a crew of assistants who are steaming and pressing every article of clothing (and there are hundreds—an entire closet's worth!). Most importantly, there's always a great photographer, too, who knows how to coax beautiful shots out of even the most unlikely of subjects. (They can make a can of cat food look glamorous.) And this photographer has a team of assistants who are setting up and tinkering with about twenty different lights, all with the end goal of making you look as flawless and perfect as possible. Preparing sets and lighting alone takes hours.

After the shoot has wrapped, the photographer will go through the hundreds and sometimes thousands of pictures snapped over the course of the day and send an edit of the best shots to the photo editor. He or she will then go through every single image with a loup (one of those magnifying eyepieces) until they find the most flawless choice. At this point, it goes to a photo retoucher, where they remove all of the unsightlies: bumps, blemishes, and stray hairs. Some magazines will even whittle arms and legs down a size or two and add some contour definition to muscles! There's an ongo-ing—and raging—debate about when to say when with the photo retouching.

Regardless, the image that ships to the newsstands is *sort of* what the person looks like—with a ton of help! Please keep this in mind when you're setting entirely unrealistic expectations for what you should look like. Celebrities and models have bad hair days, bad skin days, and bad body days, too. But their image is so con-trolled, you're never going to get to see it on a magazine cover (weeklies excluded).

ENDNOTE

I know a girl who lives in New York, who, for the longest time, had only a bed and a dresser in her apartment so that she could spend her extra money on clothing. I see the point in that: I would happily live in an empty apartment if I could fill it with shoes!

But as devoted as I may be to my wardrobe, it's important to acknowledge that true style extends beyond what you look like when you walk out the door. You don't have to express this through grand gestures, either. It's the small gestures that will really set you apart, like being gracious to waitstaff and cab drivers, holding open a door for someone who needs help, or bringing a friend flowers on her birthday.

And most importantly, it's in giving thanks. Whether it's for dinner, an informational interview, a gift, a college recommendation, or even just for being a good friend, if you're ever in doubt as to whether a thank-you note is required, write one anyway. It costs nearly nothing—save for a card and a stamp—and it's so rare that it automatically wins you major points in the class category. Plus, it *feels* good, both to write and receive one.

So to that end . . .

L

Dear friends,

Style is such a big part of my life, and I am so happy I had the opportunity to share my love for it with you. Thank you for reading my book. I hope you enjoyed it... and that you learned a few things along the way!

Best wishes,

Lauren

ACKNOWLEDGMENTS

A lot of people were involved in the making of this book, but special thanks go to:

Matt Jones, Adam Fedderly, and Tyler Jennings for working so hard to create such lovely photos, for always giving us a pink sweater to look forward to, and for listening to Disney music for two days straight.

Tara Swennen, Jennifer Teller, and Caley Lawson for going above and beyond in the styling of this book. The amount of work you put into your search for all the necessary clothing is unbelievable. We couldn't have done it without you.

Amy Nadine Rosenberg for not just making me feel beautiful, but for Disney sing-a-longs, trying weird vegetables, and getting me to take burlesque classes. I'm so lucky to be able to work with someone who is not only talented but is a dear friend.

Kristin Ess and Caitlin Rylander for working so hard to create so many fabulous 'dos and for always supplying us with a new catchphrase—"I love this story." Also for not only doing my hair but anyone else's who is within arm's reach. We end our days with the loveliest of crews.

Howard Huang and Jamie Huang for taking the time to photograph so many things and doing a beautiful job on all of them.

Elise Loehnen for making this such an enjoyable experience. It was so much fun to create this book with someone who shares my love for style.

Everyone at HarperCollins, especially Zareen Jaffery, Melinda Weigel, Cristina Gilbert, Erin Gallagher, Tom Forget, Barbara Fitzsimmons, and Elise Howard.

Melissa Bruno, who makes everything that can be exhausting about a book tour completely fun.

Farrin Jacobs and Sasha Illingworth—after two weeks of editing done in a Hyatt meeting room during a children's talent search, there are few people I would still like. But after many British clubs, multiple servings of questionable lunch meat, malfunctioning lights, crowds of maroon-clothed football fans, and more than a thousand photo kills, I'm still quite fond of you both. Go Crimson Tide!! (Hyatt, thanks for introducing me to the British club sandwich. It's pretty great!)

Matthew Elblonk for guiding me through the publishing process and taking care of the business stuff . . . or whatever. Thanks, buddy.

The wonderful team that makes it all possible: Max Stubblefield, Nicole Perez-Krueger, Teal Cannaday, and Kristin Puttkamer. To be honest, I'm running out of ways to thank you all. It's probably because you're pretty amazing at what you do. So thanks, again.

Credits

ALL PHOTOGRAPHS OF
LAUREN CONRAD

Matt Jones
(except pages 2 and 211)

ALL CLOTHING AND
PRODUCT PHOTOGRAPHS

Howard Huang
(except page 41)

FASHION STYLIST

Tara Swennen

MAKEUP

Amy Nadine Rosenberg

HAIR

Kristin Ess

ART DIRECTOR

Sasha Illingworth

Fashion Credits

On the cover and pages viii and x

Dress by Alexander Berardi; Earrings by Deszo for Roseark; Shoes by Aldo

CHAPTER 1

Page 4

Blazer by Elizabeth and James; T-shirt by Born Famous; Jeans by Hudson; Rings by Anita Ko; Bracelet by Borgioni

Page 7

Little black dress by Express; Necklace by Jennifer Meyer

Page 8

Jeans by Seven For All Mankind; Collared shirt by Theory; Necklace by Jennifer Meyer

Page 9

Skirt by Robin; Boots by Christian Louboutin

Page 10

Black top by Vince; Black heels by Christian Louboutin

Page 11

Blazer by Lauren Conrad for Kohl's; Coat by French Connection

Page 13

T-shirt by Riller and Fount; Skirt by Dolce and Gabbana; Necklace by Swarovski for Aldo

Page 14

Dress by Stella McCartney; Shoes by Christian Louboutin; Pearls by Erickson Beamon

Page 15

Polka-dot top by Geren Ford; Jeans by Levi's; Shoes by Yves Saint Laurent; Maxi dress by Cynthia Vincent; Shoes by Prada; Bracelet by Le Vian; Necklace by Danielle Stevens; Sweater by Neal Sperling; Jeans by Levi's; Boots by Chloé; Necklace by Shari Wacks

Page 16

Shoes by Christian Louboutin; Miniskirt by twenty8twelve; Blazer by Juicy

CHAPTER 2

Page 18

T-shirt by Riller and Fount; Jeans by Ever; Necklace by Sara Weinstock

225